NARCISSISTIC ROMANTICISM

notionpress
.com

NARCISSISTIC ROMANTICISM

PIYUSH ROHANKAR

notionpress.com

Notion Press

Old No. 38, New No. 6

McNichols Road, Chetpet

Chennai - 600 031

First Published by Notion Press 2015

ISBN: 978-93-5206-216-4

Dedicated to the Fairer Sex

And to the lovers of poetry...

Foreword

How does it feel to be touched by dewdrops, to be caressed on naked skin by giggling waters of a pristine stream, to be subjected to inane questions of an innocent tiddler, to find answers in warm embrace of someone you always fall back upon, to witness hide and seek of ticklish sunrays behind a canopy? You may not be able to put these experiences into words, but if you look for anything but the mundane, you somehow wish in that little corner of your heart to stay put with these events for eternity.

That is the sorcery of Piyush's craft. You may have never met these people he dedicates his odes to; they may well be the inhabitants of a distant multiverse. Chances are that you would have felt somewhat similar for someone in life or would have seen someone you know feeling that very emotion for somebody, but you could never put that into words. He does the job for you, and a splendid one at that!

Many of these poems will make you wonder how somebody could possibly write like that, and why you couldn't do that. I've already had enough of this high dudgeon. It's wonderful to have someone as talented as Piyush as your confrère. You could always use your good offices for autographs, when they get too famous.

I wish him a great career ahead; may he always becharm and bewitch us with his poesies!

Munish Sharma,
Indian Administrative Service (IAS).
Haryana Cadre.

Preface

As a person of obstinate inclination towards writing, I've always found myself gravitate towards writing in the genre of love poems and poems based on existential themes in pensive hours of musing. In my anthology of poems I talk about love and life that not only falls in the purview of the established familiar façade of ideas but one which reigns supreme even beyond the untouched domains of human consciousness.

My poems mirror feelings of deep desolation and shades of raw, morbid, sympathetic and ostensible have been presented in contradistinction. Here I celebrate women who induce awe and admiration. I have depicted the thematic evolution of love in a spectrum of 'love found, 'love lost' and 'love re-awakened' from the Victorian chivalry to the Elizabethan romance. My poems voice the myriad facets of love, love which hovers around dark abyss and that which can still capture souls through its pristine beauty. The very source of our existence that love is, I've tried to tap its varied shades in its entirety. In some poems I have tried to present the beloved through the prism of Sufi mysticism and thus taking love into the realm of religion.

The stretch of time during which these poems were composed is from the time I began my civil services preparation. Lastly, it is not without God's grace that I've been able to give form to the most pristine of emotion that love is and be able to appreciate and showcase it *au naturel*. It gives me pleasure to put forth a work which carries ineffable sentiments of awe, admiration and approbation that love and life demand and which delve deep into the chasms of our minds and hearts which are sometimes difficult to decipher. Addressing bare emotions, I hope you the reader stumbles upon the very relatable essence of it and sees the different strands of the same sentiment.

Piyush Arun Rohankar,
Asst. Collector/SDM (Officer Trainee),
DANICS, Ministry of Home Affairs,
Government of India.
29.07.15

Acknowledgements

I would like to express the deepest appreciation to my father Arun Rohankar, my mother Kalpana Rohankar and my sister Akshara Rohankar for all the love, support and blessing they have graced upon me all through my life and they still continue to do the same.

Special thanks to my fellow civil servant Amandeep Duli for the invaluable assistance in reviewing my poems patiently and helping me to explore and fine tune the various elements related to the book.

My sincere gratitude to Munish Sharma for finding my poems worthy of his endorsement.

To all my friends and admirers of my work, thank you all for the much needed motivation and love that you have showered on me always.

And finally to the many known and unknown beautiful women, who have played with my imagination to inspire me to give birth to my poems, I am forever indebted to you all, whom I humbly try to repay through my poems and would continue to do so.

Contents

To Love Her is Like a Journey

And to love her is like a journey,
Not a casual stroll or an adventure,
But a patient walk of a million miles,
And slowly her myth unfolds,
As she reveals herself in layers,
Her beauty has all the shades of life,
But I fall short of colours to paint her glory,
Oh to love her is like a journey,
A journey of a million miles…

And I am still exploring,
The darkest corners of her soul,
Of what lay beneath those eyes,
And I am still exploring,
The mysticism she practices with her smile,
Her incandescent calligraphic elegance,
Her magnetism has pulled me in her labyrinthine life,
I still walk those virgin forest she drew for me,
Where the words that kissed her lips,
Still echoes like an infectious melody,
Oh her beauty and my youth,
Had led me into believing that life would go on forever,
Oh to love her is like a journey,
A journey of a million miles…

And all the falling stars that I saw as a child,
I found them at her feet,
And my joy to watch her dance,
Over them in her Carmel.
She is the romance of a winter love story,
The picture of a million memories,
The blood of God flows through her heart,
The space in between her arms,
Is the doorway to heaven,
The light for my mornings comes from her smile,
Oh to love her is like a journey,
A journey of a million miles…

Charlotte Josephine Antoinette

A tapestry of the obscure world,
Lingering in the dark alleys of life,
So anonymous but a grammar placed to perfection,
A note so ever present but never read,
She is the love long forgotten by the roads…

A souvenir meant for nostalgia,
Wandering in the old world of catholic conscience,
So petite but a requiem to promiscuous melancholy,
The first cherries of spring reminds me of her lips,
The peaches of autumn are her cheeks,
She is the love that dwells on the long forgotten roads…

She is a religion practiced by few,
Fading fast to the plastic urban promises,
So vintage, her beauty sounds fiction,
Can't separate the maiden from the myth,
A fragrance meant for folklore,
She is the love long forgotten by the roads…

Trans-Sexual Adolescence

In those blank pages is my story,
Nothing ever written that wasn't erased,
Every thought was already a waste,
And time preserves its own memory,
A memory of me fading into time…

I carry the weight of my emptiness,
And see the world through eyes of needs,
These needs breeds more habits,
And these habits preserve my loneliness…

So don't confuse immortality with life,
For life belongs to those who can live,
We are infected with non-existence,
And there was never a cure,
We are the immortal clones of repetition…

Four walls is what remains of my kingdom now,
As history repeats itself,
We all just change names,
And the story remains the same,
You took birth inside my head,
For you are my imagination,
And I am your reality…

But reality expired long back in childhood,
A memory of 'would be could be' life we carry now,
But we still gift ourselves expectations,
And hope engulfs every illusion,
We just live on to pleasure our senses again…

You Know You Are Not Her First

And you know you are not the first,
To bite into her dimples,
And sleep in her eyes,
Whisper in her ears long deep into the nights,
But does that even matter?

And you know you are not the first,
Who had the honour of wiping her tears,
And sucking on her finger tips gently,
And taking her to bed like a child in arms,
But does that even matter?

And you know you are not the first,
Worthy of her warm hugs on winter nights,
And you know that you are not the first,
She shared her kisses and coffees,
Chocolates and love candles, shower and bed with.
But does that even matter?
Now that you have the chance of a lifetime,
To be her gardner, To be her farmer,
To resurrect the fallen princess again...

And you know you are not the first,
She gave her heart.
But does that even matter?
How you wish you would be the last,
To stay forever in her arms,
Or die waiting for that moment…

Valerie Eugenie Clementine

Let not the weight of a thousand years,
Stain your marbled skin I pray,
And let not the weight of words ever hurt,
Your delicate wine bled lips.
Wear that hallowed smile as your eternal crown,
And let it graze and let it flourish,
Let it heal my desolate heart morose,
Come and baptize all of what is left of me,
Before I wear the silence in black and white…

And what secrets of morrow,
Do you hide in your layered hair?
The constellations in your eyes,
Are asking me to explore them.
My Lady the sublime stars in the naked sky,
Are imitating your springtime waltz…

Am I drunk or am I purified?
Such a therapy your hug,
And the way you make those hair on my skin stand end to end,
By a mere touch,
Is it science or is it sorcery?

Such a surreal art you are,
An embodiment of everything beautiful that would ever be created.
I wonder what inspired God to craft you,
Was he lonely or seeking salvation…

Socially Transmitted Disease (STD)

The finest moments of my youth,
Wasted in too much of planning,
And too less of living,
Worried about the comforts of tomorrow,
And now I nurse some verses in my heart,
About my youth that has fallen apart…

All the battles of my prime,
I fought them from the confinements of my room,
Many I lost and few I won,
Only to realize it was never my war…

And now it's too late,
To let go off my loneliness,
Feels like my old age has started,
Even before my youth has faded into oblivion…

It's the winter of my youth now,
And there is no one even to hug,
The girl I longed for never came,
And all the waiting turned into,
These long and lonely hours,
Which faded into the pages of some books…

And what is left of all this learning now,
If not just worries and fears.
Now I even calculate my laughter and tears,
Carefully saving them for future,
For I have learnt to betray my feelings now,
And my hypocrisy embarrass me,
It seems to me the life of my generation,
Is some socially transmitted disease…

My Lady, This Desire is No Crime

My Lady, this desire is no crime,
To see you undress, untouched, unspoiled,
Woman your beauty is mesmerizing,
My trespassing eyes hypnotized,
As all my lust turns into ashes in your honour,
And the gravity getting heavy by your mere sight,
For I bathe in thy magnificent glory,
As you reveal inch by inch,
Of what God took seven days to make,
And I shall forfeit the seven heavens,
To possess what lays beneath your beautiful breast,
And lay to rest in those jade green eyes,
With your heart inside mine,
As the stars slide down your hair into my eyes.
So undress beneath the interstellar lights,
For none shall see but just my eyes,
And none shall feel but just my heart,
So hide no more in your coyness,
For you are an artwork supreme,
My Lady, this desire is no crime,
To watch you undress, untouched, unspoiled…

Her Cigarettes and Beers

The way you philosophize life,
With those beer tins in your hand,
Lady, such a poetry you are when you are drunk,
And those cigarettes in between your pretty fingers,
You look so very graceful when you are smoking,
So very beautiful in the haze,
Like some medieval artwork,
So worthy to be on canvas…

I just love to watch you struggle in bed,
Fighting the sunlight with your pillow,
And in all the glory of your Sunday morning hangover,
Innocence oozes out of your drunken face,
And Oh my Godless lady it's time for your,
Lemonades, Novocain and hour long shower in silence.
I know it's crazy to believe in silly things,
But you look so very pure when you suffer from your addictions…

The Lonely Traveller

The mirror betrays my thoughts,
I see myself but I am lost,
Searching for a memory,
But remembrances they fade…

The words in my diaries,
No longer preserve my youth,
So alone in those paragraphs,
So faceless in those photographs,
These scarlet lines on my palms,
Are as aimless as my life…

I see hope on the horizon,
And beginning of another illusion,
For every tune that once echoed from long,
Turned out to be the same melancholic song…

The void within is fathomless,
As bottomless as the universe,
Even my shadow is ashamed of my loneliness,
I see my life is no different,
Than those tables and chairs,
Kept waiting for nothing…

So I sat beneath a tree to figure out my life,
But all I was left covered with was fallen leaves.
With every breath we fade into nothingness,
This is all that has ever been there to life,
No more no less…

So I keep drifting on my destiny quietly,
Puppet of an indifferent time,
I wonder will I be just another story,
Meant to be forgotten before time…

Primal Feelings

A beauty that dwells in forbidden thoughts,
That echoes in the pages of myths,
I know that she exist somewhere in between,
The unconscious realm of feelings,
For my heart magnifies her traces subtle,
Her essence found in everything beautiful and gentle,
From sea shells to church bells,
They speak about her presence.
For crusades a many have been taken,
To establish her existence.
Her life still a riddle,
On every philosopher's quest…

But what misses the eye,
Has been caught by feelings.
A light house of hope,
In my heart keeps burning.
My eyes dying to see,
What my heart has known for years.
Or am I foolish to give her a physical form,
And enslave her in this world gone wrong…

A feeling that she is of spring making love,
To the trees green and the doves,
The same feeling of lying naked on the grass,
And watch the rain falling from the stars.
A feeling that she is that walks in and slips away,
Like the sand of an hourglass.
Oh her home the realm of feelings…

Noushafarin Esfahani

I die a thousand deaths when you fail to acknowledge my existence,
I live a thousand lives, all at once, when you look my way and smile,
Life and death is devoid of any meaning in your absence,
My eyes search for the light that rises from you…

Just like the flowers,
Who have forgotten autumn and winter,
Oh my friend from past seven seasons,
Have you forgotten me,
Like the many names in your life?
Or are you busy loving yourself,
Trapped in your own enchantment are you?
How many autumns more, oh the wait…

I don't know where you dwell,
But the shortest way to you is through my dreams,
I don't know where you dwell,
But the surest way to find you is inside my head,
And I will meet you there…

Existential Menopause

....And so many dreams have died in my bed,
It smells of my past which hasn't slept,
And God only knows who sleeps in my place,
My eyes close and another life begins...

The morning light splits my eyes into two,
Still confused if the day is worth getting up to,
I wonder what new did I ever do?
Except staring blankly into the blue,
And making stories inside my head,
None of which shall ever come true...

So I have lived long enough to see,
What time has done to me,
I remember by name all bruises on my body,
And each scar is just the same story,
Those tattoos have faded into wrinkles,
Still living with all that is left of me...

And maybe someday on my rocking chair,
I would be a man of memories and grey hair,
I will still wonder if my life was worth it,
Worth every breath that faded into monotony,
And maybe I will still lie one last time,
Celebrate everything that was lost and applause,
To escape this long recurring Existential Menopause…

Anne

I like to watch her bathe,
In the million morning drops of yellow,
Falling from the half-baked sunday morning sun,
And I am so jealous of the pillows and bed sheets and winds,
For they get to kiss her where ever they feel.
And the day has just begun, oh I wonder,
If the universe conspires,
To make her look so beautiful…

Someday I will bargain hard,
To get bitten and kissed by her tender lips,
And preserve that scar as a sign of God.
How I wish that winter would last forever,
So that I could offer myself to keep her warm,
And wrap her around like a child in my arms.
But now I know for sure,
The only reason winter doesn't last forever,
Because even summer and spring are waiting to love her too…

A Portrait of Timelessness

Subdued by your beautiful timelessness,
Mesmerized by the elegance that dawn bestows on you.
Captivated by what the first light from heaven,
Does to your unkempt hair.
Enchanted by the way morning dresses you in innocence,
Mellowed by the best my eyes have ever seen,
For your face melts in every eyes,
And reaches the heart in no time...

Then you become a picture within,
And follow people in every thought,
Now they are reading stars to know your story,
And studying constellations to know your location,
For you are someone inside their head,
They long to feel and preserve...

For your face belongs to every age,
And every royalty would fight I know,
To own your divine legacy.
But sleep only with the angels my lady,
May your God be your best lover...

And if your feather feet ever touch,
This crying and bleeding earth,
Walk gently through haste and waste,
And wait patiently for your religion to take birth,
For people from world beyond,
Are meant to be prayed and loved…

A Foreword to Existential Paradox

With every desire I am born again,
Every unfulfilled desire keeps me alive,
For I am a man with many lives,
I wonder which one is really mine...

And what is a circle if not a mere repetition of a single line,
In essence our life is no different than that circle,
Watch closely as time's hands are drawing year after year,
Your circle across mine...

And remember it's a sin not to feel,
But what has been felt,
Should always be forgotten,
For if you remember how it feels,
The feelings won't feel the same again...

And learn how to unlearn the past,
Remember no more than how to breathe,
The more you are lost and all alone,
The more of yourself you can own...

And nothing is alright for long,
For nothing should be alright for long,
And if it is then something is wrong,
For how long are you going to play the same old song?

And if you live long enough you will know,
Your truth is someone else's lie.
So love and live knowing perfectly well,
Everything that appears and reappears is not what it is…

And as your eyes are ever present but not the light,
So at dawn do remember last night,
For far there is also a world of shadows and twilight,
That you will never know if you only believe your eyes…

Dearest Wife

Along a path for years I waited patiently,
I destroyed my reputation in search for your love,
I traded my life for more glasses of wine,
But no sleep would ever be waiting for me,
Until the hour that made you mine…

Those long lost years were worth the wait,
And here I am now in your possession.
I hold your hand and I never feel low,
I am wedded to your shadow too, you know…

For I am a fan of everything that leaves your lips,
Smiles, kisses, abuses and anger,
Every bit of you makes me feel younger,
And every passing day I lust for more of you…

Forever and eternity doesn't sound enough my lady,
To measure my love in length and breadth of time,
So I am finding ways to make your heart hear,
But all I can do now is smile and leave a tear…

So believe me when I say I love you,
How much and how long are questions,
Whose answers are in my hugs and kisses,
For every hug would mean the rest of your age,
And every kiss is an ocean of love in which we float…

I Love You

I'll run my fingers across your stomach,
Draw a circle round your belly button,
Run my stubble down your neck,
I'll bless those cheeks with a kiss,
And whisper in your ears I love you…

I'll run my nose through your hair,
Bite the bottom of your ears,
Press your nails across my skin,
And hear me through your silence,
As I say I love you…

And as you sleep in your deepest of dreams,
It's still middle of the night,
I'll stay awake late to watch you sleep,
Will get close enough to hear you breathe,
I'll keep warm by inhaling what you exhale,
And hear me through the silence of your sweetest dreams,
Quietly as I whisper in your ears I love you…

Faded Libido

Every passing day I am a shadow of yesterday,
As nameless as any other passer-by,
While slowly life leaks away and time passes by,
Only responsibilities and wrinkles multiply,
And destiny is all that is left as an alibi…

The feelings blunt out as blades of grass,
The libido mellows into old age and pass,
All life leaves us with is a blurry sight,
And a future as bright as fading light…

I feel now like a cigarette in a dustbin,
In two minds about everything,
Educated only to procrastinate,
Until tomorrow as always,
As my mind wanders endlessly…

Chasing something never meant to last,
As permanence is just another mirage,
Time only waits for you in photographs,
And life shall always have the last laugh…

Don't remember anything that was truly mine,
Suffocated by the feeling that my life never rhymed,
And now there is a full stop at the end of every line.
But the problem starts when you think you can be happy,
For nothing ever waits except for death...

Her 7th Dunhill International

...And it's her 7th Dunhill International,
In those polka dotted underwear,
Tattered hair and tube socks to pair,
Listening to metal, her little way to rebel,
And it's just seven in the morning,
Waiting for the sun,
To clear her clouded eyes,
I wonder if she would dissolve in her tears.
It seems those adolescent kisses,
Ended up in heartbreak again.
All those coffees have turned into sour kisses,
And now her black smoked eyes,
Are searching for an escape,
In those bottles of Vodka.
I wonder if she would flirt with spirituality again,
And renew her pledge to purify,
To bleach out her life from darkness.
Now in some chamber of her heart,
She is burning memories of another stranger,
Clearing the drawers in her mind,
Of the same old poetries of love.
But even in this coldness of her rubble,

When her heart is in ruins,
Such a beautiful mess she is.
That's her life in black and white,
And her 7th Dunhill International again...

Claire Mary Augustine

You intrude my sorrow and rain serenity,
And grant me passage into tranquillity,
And on the parchment of my life,
So often you leave an autograph with your smile...

And when our smiles meet I become speechless,
My pen becomes wordless by thy sight,
So I choose silence in your presence,
Oh! The joy to watch you without judgment...

The prophetic talents of your heart I don't understand,
The wisdom you contain is so different than mine,
My mortal intelligence cannot fathom your beauty,
So I break my pen so as not to be judged of heresy...

Only through you I can experience eternity,
Or understand the meaning of infinity,
For at your gates the time begs you to decide its fate,
Or have mercy on its many defects...

I don't seek an explanation to your divine mystery,
For I know the limits of my knowledge.
All I seek is the patronage of your mercy,
And refugee in the depths of your eyes…

The Plague

With an empty stare the time watches me,
Questions me about my hollow existence,
I say let my heart bleed itself peacefully,
As I pass into oblivion…

These sterile feelings which I left for dead,
Have woken up from their grave,
My heart forlorn, my dying dreams,
And my shadow owns this loneliness…

As I battle this plague from past,
I pin my hope in your sacred grace,
Thy love shall resurrect itself I know,
In the most unholiest of places…

And when your smile clears,
The fear from my eyes,
And I find myself still alive,
I know,
It's just the beginning of all that ends…

A Girl Without A Cure

I wonder what went wrong with her,
That's too much of Chanel N°5 and far too less clothes,
And nothing left to the imagination,
As winter spreads its icy wings everywhere.
I wouldn't advice those high heels either,
If you down a quarter of Jack Daniel's all by yourself,
And why wouldn't she listen to her mom?
I wonder what went wrong...

I wonder why she hides her pretty eyes,
Behind those Wayfarers, it's such a waste,
Is it sadness or the neon lights?
I wouldn't advice asking strangers for a light,
If you are that pretty and drunk,
And why wouldn't she listen to her mom?
I wonder what went wrong...

And now I hear rumours about her,
Of how she steals time from men,
Of how they overdose on her,
And never get cured, never recover.
The streets are full of her stories,
And so are the asylums.
I wonder why wouldn't she stop and get clean,
But Alas! She says she never had a mom,
To tell her what's right from wrong…

Resurrection Chant

In the faceless fields the nameless yields,
With time the fallen and forgotten heals,
And very soon the joy of moaning shall begin,
For the rotten happiness of an unapologetic past,
Has come to reside in their broken hearts…

Shall come to pass the weather of failure,
As hopes exposes itself in layers,
What winter loses is springs gain,
The dawn shall seek the dark again…

Shall rise in silence what are meant to fall,
Failure is only the beginning of the resurrection's call,
When the faithless in happiness shall rule all,
The symbols will crumble and love shall gain…

Far away from the living the blessed live,
The elysian fields are just a grave away,
As sooner or later when the silence fall,
Death is nature's best gift to all,
Where the worthy shall live forever in grace…

Obsessive Compulsive Love

In a desert full of echoes,
Surrounded by vast ocean of empty time,
I live a life so very blind,
That all I see is you…

For every thought walks me back into you,
And to you it all returns my undying love,
I stretch my mind to the farthest shore,
And all I hear is your lore…

Now all that is left of education for me,
Is to read and write your name,
Those blank pages invite me evermore,
To fill them over and over,
With your memories that ever grows…

And although my life is not a blessing,
I still bless your name,
For whatever little joy in my life that is left,
It is left in hearing your name…

Broken Vows

Come my dearest, Come my darling,
Come the father of baroque church is calling,
Come like the bride on whom the white roses are falling,
Oh come just to break your vows again…

Come like the memory of the forgotten,
That lines up in silence,
Come out from your graveyard,
Dug deep within my heart,
Oh come on a gentle winter Vivaldi violin tune,
Like a subtle remembrance…

Come my maiden to the silent convent,
Hidden deep within the mountain of saints,
Come my maiden to the medieval bell,
Near the Romanesque village wishing well,
Oh come I wait for you lonely here,
Oh come just to break your vows you made there…

Come and infect me,
With the happiness you suffer from.
Come and bring me,
To the point of tears.
Come and haunt me,
I wait here lonely.
Oh come just to break your vows again…

Orphans of Yesterday

Success hides what failure reveals,
But nothing ever learnt from either,
The illusion just lasts too long,
And by the time it's over,
The reality gets written in the pages of history,
While slowly time weaves our story…

We lose more than we ever gain,
But this lust just never ends,
So gather whatever you may today,
Before time comes and takes everything away…

Hope is a mask that time wears to pass away,
As happiness is a blatant lie of life,
Concealed from us right from our birth.
Wait for your life to begin my friend,
For life starts only after it hurts…

In all my stupidities I truly felt free,
While in my senses I felt chained,
But I am too old to realize this now,
Civilized beyond my permission to be a slave…

We are the legacy of our bloodline,
By the time our forefathers realized how helplessly they were lost,
We were born and raised.
And now we walk the same old roads of perdition,
On our way to become orphans of yesterday…

The Long Promiscuous Wait

With the love she has to offer,
She hopes to buy some warmth.
You see, it's a cold place to be,
And the pretty face is on her own…

And every man she loved,
She thought it would be her last.
The faces they kept changing,
But not her promiscuous past…

She lives the same old story,
Of promises that were never meant to be,
She knows she better hurry,
Before the sun sets on her youthful hue…

She knows what she has to offer,
To get a taste of life that is best,
But without love this bargain won't last long,
Still she hasn't learnt it from others mouth…

I offered my love wrapped in words,
But she knew she could do much better than just words.
And now she is in love again,
Undressed in the arms of another man…

And for me to see all this,
A strange happiness crosses my mind,
For I wait patiently for her heart to get broken,
So I could beg at her doorsteps again…

The Boy Who Wanted To Be Your Man

He was just a boy begging to you,
To the woman that you already were.
The boy you were never good to,
Who wanted to grow old with you.
You could have helped him with his life,
But all he had was love to give,
And you bet on the promises of those foreign men,
Busy buying those dreams,
From lips you wouldn't have otherwise kissed,
But all your best laid plans,
Ended up in eleven days and twelve night stand,
And followed by such fantasies again…
Maybe it was your age speaking back then,
But before you wore those rented looks,
On the way to your same old unguided mistakes,
Didn't those love poems he wrote for you,
Even once meant anything to you?
Didn't those songs he played for you on his faded guitar,
Ever split your heart into two?
Or were you busy buying those foreign dreams,

From lips you wouldn't have otherwise kissed,
But now all your best laid plans,
Ended up in tears and cans,
And it pains now even without loving.
Do you remember that boy,
Who wanted to be your man?

In Search of Indifference

To a life I never asked for,
To a life that is slowly leaving me,
To a death that is still a dream,
I have made peace with everything…

To a name I didn't even choose,
To a name that doesn't sound mine,
But it stays and lives in my place,
To a name of a nameless face,
I have made peace even with you…

And nothing makes me smile,
Nothing but the worst fears of mine,
The dying of my dreams is what I dream,
And in those dreams I live evermore…

And to a start and to an end,
If ever you exist except inside my head,
Know that time ceaselessly walks uninvited,
Towards an ending for a new beginning of another end…

To the few memories that were granted to me,
Has outlived its purpose to cherish them anymore,
And with its passage life teaches us nothing else,
But indifference towards life itself and death that awaits…

The Bridal Princess

If she had but time and world enough,
To conquer and rule,
She would have with ease,
All the seven heavens and beyond,
With her sweetest of curve,
Her crimson smile,
And those marshmallow lips,
The symbol of her empire,
The jewel of time,
And when she lifts her bridal veil,
She leaves a seal,
On every amoral heart to heal.
She feels so cotton,
And her velvet fingers,
Holding those Tulips in ribbons,
And the calmness that grace her face,
Are these the omen of prosperity and peace?

Her Tranquil Vinyl voice,
And the sparkle in her vintage eyes,
Are the canons of beauty,

And the pearls in her ears,
Reminds me of the stars from Celtic twilight.
Look how intimately the nature imitates her,
And gently blends into her existence…

Now I am no more than what she makes me feel,
I feel no more than what I see in her,
I see the world only through her eyes,
For I am no more than a name if not for her,
My lines have already been drawn,
In her pristine existence.
For she can stop my clock,
And change my time into space,
And I can feel all this,
Without an ounce of spirit…

She is so dew and dove,
In that crown and gown,
Of floral lattice and laces,
Oh she is the love of the ages,
The Bridal Princess…

Elizabeth Madeline Spencer

Heavy on my mellow mind,
A yellow sombre melodic maiden,
Laid out like a surreal sonnet on a grand Baldwin,
She touches that part of my grey,
Long lost to the struggles of time…

All my feeling are now dipped and soaked,
In her heathen existence,
And all my servile pain vanish by the fragrance,
Of her heaven scented hairs of gold.
She is the prologue to the long promised spring in my life,
An epitaph to my existential monochrome…

All miracles are not mysteries but she is one,
For I see the papal prophecy of a messenger in her.
Oh passer-by, but let not her smile deceive you,
Into believing that you can possess her too,
For she was here long before you,
For she would be here long after you turn into ashes,
For she is no one's, yet everyone's to love…

An Exercise in Repetition

The days do see my sorrow multiply,
At times the sun does shine on my joy,
But for far too little I'm staking so much,
The best of what I had has been lost to time...

Not often my heart skips the seconds as I grow,
Such moments are so far and few to show,
And now as indifference grows on my brow,
It pains the most when I don't feel anything...

I do leave my bed to see tomorrow,
And traverse the landscape that my desires paint,
But every night when I return to my bed,
My existence seems to be a mere exercise in repetition...

Our desires make us chase mirage on the horizon,
This world is a riddle of our imagination,
To keep or to leave means the same with age,
As one day you will find we don't mean much to time,
And this loop is what you call life...

Into Her Arms

That one face I pray that should never change,
Which takes me to bed every night,
And locks me up in her arms with her gentle might,
And puts me to sleep amidst the ruins of a fading light…

That one face I pray that should never age,
Who crossed my path and stayed on my page,
And saved me from my youth's rave and rage,
For all painless nights I owe to her beautiful gaze…

To that one face whose eyes sing me to sleep,
And gently walks me into her garden of dreams,
She is my nest, to which I return faithfully every single night,
And every single night she gives me life that day takes away…

If not for those kisses that she plants on me,
The bruises that time leaves would never heal,
And I surrender to the warmth of her embrace,
As she teaches me how to feel and let go of things…

Scarred By Her

No woman would ever touch me,
Because they know my history,
That once I was your territory.
And no woman would ever trespass into me,
For they still think of me as your property…

No woman would ever explore me,
For nothing is left in me for them to claim.
They still think of you when they think of me,
For they know how brutally you loved me once…

You have scarred me for a lifetime,
Even the angels won't take me without your permission.
I'm your leftover they say,
And I'm all yours to keep…

Consensual Mourning

Not one pleasure left,
That doesn't lead to disappointment.
The price too high as ever,
To belong somewhere,
And my pain thus as always,
People leave and memories remain…

God gifted me this life,
But the days pass by without a choice,
And to keep discovering the same old things,
Oh to find myself on the verge of nowhere.
I keep reminding my loneliness,
Everything is but just a passing phase…

Ashamed of what I do in the name of living,
Nothing excites me more than what is yet to come,
And for this moment I wait day after day.
Another day just walked by,
Leaving no memory of itself as it leaves.

Dreaming of what the coming days might look like.
It's just me counting my days and they all look the same,
So much so that I have stopped counting them.
Remember today for this is how the rest of your life will look like...

Juliet Ceaser

She came, She saw, She conquered,
And how easily I surrendered,
Without even giving a fight,
So blinded was I by her radiant light,
She pierced my heart with a single touch,
Her bewitching eyelashes and whispering smile,
Left me paralyzed for a while,
And when I came back to my senses,
I was tied to her scent and prisoner of her will,
She keeps me blindfolded with her hair,
So I just follow where ever she goes,
And now she shall have it all,
My sleep, my smile,
All the dreams I have been dreaming for a while,
And she shall have it all,
My nights and my days,
All my secrets and my ways,
And what is it that hides now,
Behind those doors of time?
I wonder and I pray,
Will she let me stay or throw me away,
Before she leaves for another quest.
She came, She saw, She conquered…

Her Guilty Pleasure

Sitting beneath the Nazi Cross,
Counting all her past lovers,
Whose names she barely remembers,
I wonder, to her, if they are just a number,
For her smile widens with every count,
Her favorite pass time post bedtime,
Feeling guilty to what she did to them,
But the smile refuses to fade,
For God, innocently she says, will forgive her and all her guilty pleasures,
Because that's his duty to do so…

Her wine soaked lips,
And fingers playing with olives,
Are still counting all the winter promises she broke,
And it's so easy for her,
To win them over,
Only to break their heart again,
And the pleasure she takes,
In those final hugs and goodbye kisses, her victory march.
For God, innocently she says, will forgive her and all her guilty pleasures,
Because that's his duty to do so…

Amongst the Unknown

Take back your victory, undo your trying,
No more prayers to the dead and the dying,
In the kingdom of forgotten it's all the same,
The purest of truth in mirror has no name,
We are the first amongst the unknown…

The believers sing the holy songs of fear,
Virgin silence has long bled to tears,
Fear no more child the mother says,
You shall be safe again in another grave…

Clean the grass from earth's breast,
Wine bled sky has opened the flood gates.
So we now take the gift of suffering,
And return what was not ours in his sacred games,
Wear no more than the skin we borrowed,
The Gods prefer us naked in the judgment hours…

Rest in Peace

She rests in peace somewhere in heaven,
As I am still counting the years, it has been seven,
Of what made her happy back then is now hurting me much,
As I delve through her memories here on earth,
Dear Lord this love should never have taken birth.
Of what made her happy back then is now hurting me much.
Heaven bound my eyes, for her as I search,
Alas the clouds, they burry her deep,
As she rests in peace somewhere in heaven...

To forget easily is not a gift I am blessed with,
The winters and those valentines,
I did my loving all the time,
But now the difference,
She sits in heaven with saint valentine,
And here I am on my borrowed time.
The only way, I imagine,
She is still around and mine
And I know for sure those signs,
Dark are the days when she never smiles,
Dead are the seasons,

When she never dances for a while.
Oh to forget easily is not a gift I am blessed with,
Of what made her happy back then is now hurting me much,
As she now rests in peace somewhere in heaven…

Live, Don't Leave!

Have you decided to skip,
The rest of your life,
For a place up there?
Dearest the girl there is nothing,
Nothing up there,
No kingdom in the clouds,
No promised land for angels,
No garden of flowers for you,
And if you leave will you ?
Will you come down again?
As rain from the sky,
To say goodbye?
Live, please don't leave,
It's not the season of fallen leaves,
It's not the hour to grief,
No one love stories which are brief,
What's the point to leave?
When it's time to live.
There is no hurry in heaven,
No time runs up there,
Even the Gods have a disease,
Boredom they say.
Live, please don't leave,

No river of wine flows up there,
No water too pure to cure your sins,
No land too holy to die for,
Live, don't leave…

2001-1899

Although the voice inside my head says otherwise,
As if I ever had a choice?
Now addicted to the very things I never wanted,
I will miss the pain if it ever leaves me and go,
I will celebrate it in my memories I know…

The idea of being free scares me now,
Seeking comfort in this web of relationships and how,
Falling in love just to get hurt over and again,
For nothing ever makes me feel alive than this pain…

The duality in our existence,
Is the very essence of our life,
The repetition of contradiction,
Is a condition of life.
So let it go, don't hold on too tight,
If you won't say goodbye,
You will never have a story to tell…

The journey is to find our way back to the start,
And seek the future in our past,
For far into the distance I see someone like me,
Trying to figure out the same old lie that life is…

Esra

Hidden in the air,
The feeling slowly grows,
And then the haunting starts,
Like some whispering in the dark,
Intoxicating the mind,
And then I know it's time,
To worship her shrine…

For far beyond the limitations of my imagination,
A place where time refuses to touch her,
I have kept her tied with the threads of love,
And though I keep forgetting my prayers to God,
God will forgive me I know,
For I worship her five times a day,
Seven days a week religiously…

I Can But Only Imagine

What do I know?
Of how your lips taste,
And how your kisses heal,
And how your hugs feel.
What do I know of how it feels?
To drown in your eyes,
And to rest in your arms.
I can but only imagine…

Oh! To the one who I can never possess,
I bring to you my loneliness,
Don't walk away knowing my pain,
For I have walked far from myself,
There is no returning to me without you…

And what do I know?
Of how your cheeks taste,
And how your hair smell,
And how your soul feels.
What do i know of how it feels?
To hold your hand,
And to kiss your petite feet.
I can but only imagine…

Oh! To the one who I can never possess,
But who possess me unwillingly!
We both know my love for my helplessness,
I prefer the emptiness you have blessed me with,
For nothing ever grows in my barren heart except you…

Oh! To the one who I can never possess,
Before you go let me know,
Which meadows harbour your fragrance,
And which flowery petals are replicas of your lips.
For what do I know of your origin?
I can but only imagine and imagine…

The Age of Lust

The things I love,
And the things I hate,
Are all inside my head,
Still not content with what I waste,
And whatever pleases me I chase.
So when do I stop this haste?

My senses they torment me,
Tired to feed them all the time.
A taste of past they seek,
As if it would be any better the next time…

I fear a future that I cannot grasp,
As I bargain myself through this life.
My promises are fantasies which I sell and buy,
And the more I lust the more I lie,
The more I become a stranger in my own eye…

My Little Juliet

A six year old,
And my love for her,
You may think otherwise,
But I don't care.
And for the pure hearted,
Please read on,
My friendship with her
Hasn't been that long…

Her love for peppermints and play cards,
Her curiosity for things for the way they are,
Her shyness to show her new stickers that glow,
And those questions she answers,
With her "I don't know" smile…

Her obsession for fairytales,
Cartoons and crayons in her pockets,
She gifts a smile to anyone and everyone
Who brings her a chocolate…

For a grownup like me,
To learn from her,
What it takes to love,
It comes naturally to her…

Her curiosity that speaks has tricked my mind,
Her ignorance and innocence has warmed my heart.
And the jealousy and envy in me,
I wonder what I search in her,
In her short and innocent life.
Is it the past of mine?
Or the person that I will never be…

Renaissance

The death of innocence in the womb of wisdom.
This sudden enlightenment is just another ignorance.
This happiness is cursed, an eternal thirst,
The rootless are blessed,
The rest fight someone else's war…

Look deep inside your loneliness,
Renaissance begins in emptiness,
The revival of the lost,
Is just another escape from ourselves…

With every breath we can end it all,
The gift of life is not for all,
But our long bloodless crawl,
Like kings without a quest,
The real romance is in this feeling of death…

Her Crown of Scarf

Busy painting the trees green,
To bring back her spring,
You make the snow look so pale,
Do you belong to some fairy tale?

Her path leads through the heart,
From where it is apart,
Which she mends, her art,
Using ancient spell,
She rings the heart's bell…

A crown of scarf she wears,
Prettiest of the pretty little princess,
Now desires taking roots deep within,
To be the next holy queen,
Of believers and non-believers alike…

As she kneels down to pray,
To Allah she has something to say,
Falling on her the golden rays,
Heaven sent, the blessing is shining,
On her crown, the holy scarf…

Molested Evolution

First they kill the child in you,
And then teach you how to live,
But I can't pretend that child is dead,
I was once a child and ever since I have been one,
I tried telling them but they won't listen…

I could never make sense to them,
They only heard what they wanted to hear,
And now I am so full of fear,
Because that's all they wanted me to feel.
They loved only when I was in tears,
Because that's only when God hears.
I shouldn't say this but I have started to think i am sick,
I am just a sheep that followed the rod and the stick…

I miss having conversations with someone I used to be,
For now they planted thoughts of people long dead,
I don't even get to choose who stays inside my head,
And all that remains of childhood now,
Are faded pages of vague memory.

Suffer now they said for a better distant life,
It's a lie I need to believe in because everyone else does.
And I wonder if self-control means waiting?
Because that's the only thing I have ever done…

Catherine

The smile has left your lips,
And it's traveling towards me,
And God only knows now,
Where it will take me.
Whether it will take me back,
And leave me in the whispering forest of my childhood memories,
Or amidst the silent springtime light,
Falling gently on the pleasant waves,
Of the coast of the Aegean Sea…

I follow the sound of your anklets,
To find my way.
I seek your shadow to feel protected.
And patiently I wait for the winds,
To gently kiss your hair playfully,
And reveal those earrings my lucky charm,
And in that nose ring you wear,
You look like a beauty from another time…

And your eye lashes do that to me every now and then,
Make my heart skip a beat.
Do that to me often so I can,
Complain to God about this life being so short,
And beg him for another life time besides you…

And now that the smile has left your lips,
And it's traveling towards me,
And God only knows now,
Where it will take me…

Her Silence

Will I find a place in your memory?
Or if you choose to write a story,
I wonder if you will remember?
Or will I be your forgotten December?

Is this your final goodbye?
These seven days of silence,
How am I supposed to read it?
Should I wait for more silence to follow,
Some more patience to swallow?
Is this your final goodbye?
How can I hear you
From the calls you aren't picking up?
Your words that are hard to come by,
Through the letters you aren't replying
Tell me how can I see you,
Through this veil of silence?

Your pictures from the past,
They refuse to speak now,
They tell a different story now,
Of what they used to back then,
Have the sweet grapes of love turned sour?
Why this silence at this point of hour?

What words should I choose?
To break this silence that grows evermore,
Tell me, what words should I choose?
To end this emotional abuse.
What went wrong in your heart?
That you are falling apart,
Oh lets go back to the start.

Will I find a place in your memory?
Or if you choose to write a story,
I wonder if you will remember?
Or will I be your forgotten December?

Anonymous Since

If not my own fantasy then,
Whose imagination am I?
Not a day goes by wondering,
Where exactly am I?
Inside my head or inside your eye…

If not my own myth then,
Whose fiction am I?
Am I more than just a name,
Or just an unknown number,
In the long forgotten government records…

If not my own conclusion then,
Whose reality am I?
Lost in the endless sea of nameless faces.
Once I wanted to conquer the world,
Now I am having a hard time even holding on to myself…

And then I realize I was in the wrong lane altogether,
The journey was never about knowing this world,
It was always about knowing our self,
And so it seems this journey will never get over,
For we will never truly know who we really are,
And I wonder if you can argue otherwise…

Let Her Be Loved

Let there be love and let her be loved,
No matter whose lips it comes from,
No matter whose kisses she accepts,
Let her be loved....

Let her flower gracefully,
No matter which garden she chooses to be in,
No matter which season it is,
No matter who the gardener is,
Let there be admirers and lovers at her doorsteps,
Let there be worshipers at her feet,
Let there be love and let her be loved...

Let there be someone always,
To bring her smiles and roses,
To hold her hand, to clear her tears,
No matter who she decides to hug in her fears,
No matter in whose arms she decides to take shelter,
Let there be love and let her be loved...

The Quest

Loosen the sense of despair,
Hasten the fall of fear,
Speak out the verse forbidden,
And embrace the love of the obvious…

Feel the bewitchment of silence,
Stop the negotiations within,
Give up the armistice with failure,
When everything is lost which was meant to be,
And now all that remains is you…

The one pregnant with pain,
Gains with abortion of revenge,
Unfear death, unfear the leaving,
It's just a foreplay of your mind…

The asylum for the guilty,
Heaven and her colony Hell,
Are just another assumption of fear.
The blessing of an honorable death,
Is the best gift of life for the worthy…

Avantika

The history of human salvation reads,
She is well known for her gratitude,
And although marked for silence amongst her equals,
The grace in her tongue makes her more than me and you…

The clarity with which she captures the moment,
Are visible in her humble words and acts.
The depth of purification that her soul has reached,
Is written all over her smile.
But she knows her biggest weakness is mercy,
As a cold time imposes on her generosity…

She suffers from excess of modesty,
She speaks so plain and her vow of poverty,
But sooner or later she would claim,
Her birth right to be an angel again,
But as of now there are other demands of her time…

I want no fate other than what is written by her,
For I believe in her providence.
And even if my heart is meant to be broken,
I want her to do that honour,
For I pray to her to grant me a warm ending…

Emmanuelle

Something changes slowly inside,
By a mere whisper of your voice,
Or just by an illusion of it,
And then it becomes difficult,
To break this spell,
That leaves me paralyzed,
In the entanglement of your cryptic smile,
I find myself ever tied…

If your photographs can make me shiver,
Even In the warmth of a burning wax.
If just a simple glance from you,
Can destroy the difference between,
Night and day and the time in between,
And I even fear to look into those beautiful brown eyes,
Are those eyes doors to another realm?
What if I get lost in them forever?
I fear to imagine all the things that you can do to me,
By a mere touch of your skin…

Societal Schizophrenia

I am scared to look inside me,
Except me everyone else is in here,
And they said education was the cure,
Now of not even one thing that I am sure…

And my heart I have been cheating,
With all these religious teachings.
My freedom is in their slavery,
These preachers are worse than butchers…

And all my emotions are hijacked,
Because the majority says so,
And the minority says no,
It's all about their fight,
And never about my rights…

Which hands should I kiss?
And whose feet should I seek?
Which religion should I sleep with,
To marry the love I care for…

Should I touch and feel?
Or would it be a sin?
Never mind I'll learn this feeling,
From mouths that have never felt anything…

Who put those words in our mouth,
And these dreams in our head,
That we carry to our bed.
Whose emotions are we feeling?
And whose life are we living?
There is confusion within confusion,
As to why we are confused.
And now we lie even without knowing about it…

The Love Beneath My Skin

Switch off the light, Step inside my life,
The Shadows are dead, My heart was bled…

See me now through the eyes of death,
Love me now with your every breath…

Take this blade and carve my heart,
Love me now in this fluorescent red…

Peel off my skin in layers and look within,
Feel me now to the core in your bones…

Dig in deep for salvation and grace,
Make my body your eternal grave…

Morbid Love

Watch me closely, slowly I am dying,
Do you still love me? And my decaying smile…

Before they dress me in black,
And leave me in abyss to rot,
Hug me one last time,
And through my icy cold breathing,
Hear my deceased heart saying,
Darling I will love you deep,
From my eternal chamber of sleep…

My angel mistress I kneel before thee,
Kiss my melting lips with passion,
And make them blood red like you used to,
Before I say goodbye to light,
And goodbye to grace…

And if you ever remember my grave my love,
Leave some flowers, letter and kisses,
To keep me warm in your memories,
I shall wait patiently to meet you again…

Soldier Without A War

Conversion is no cure for the numberless,
The slumber of ignorance shall prevail,
From harvest to harvest the land remains red,
The sacred games shall once again be played…

Who you see in mirror is lonely,
Reflections are nothing but a work of truth,
We are the soldiers without a war,
Betrayed once again by the lines…

For today has become part again,
Of clocks and calendars and prayers.
And future is a dark labyrinth,
To the lost crown of yesterday.
Where shall we seek salvation now?
For past is but the heritage of few.
We are the soldiers without a war,
In the blank pages of some folklore…

Lady Emine

The four book says,
The passage to heaven lay,
Through your kajal clad eyes,
And salvation within the doors of your heart.
Oh it's a long pilgrimage into you,
But I am here, your believer,
As I kiss your holy feather feet,
A thousand times as a prayer and wait,
For you to lift the veil and let me in,
Your eyes, a labyrinth,
A walk through a silent forest,
Where time stops still,
Your eyes where I meet my childhood.
Guided by angels,
I keep walking into those eyes,
Not knowing when I would reach,
At the door steps of your heart,
And I would wait there till eternity,
Because I don't know where else to go.
My promised land, your heart,
I am here, your believer,
As I kiss your holy feather feet,
A thousand times as a prayer and wait,
For you to lift the veil and let me in,
Oh it's a long pilgrimage into you…

Cocaine

All she need is someone,
To buy her all her fun,
She looks so happy in that smile,
She is content all the while,
But she knows deep within her heart,
It won't last her all the mile...

But she still wears up her smile,
As if her world was all happy and fine,
She is on the lookout for the game,
Her wild heart she cannot tame,
For her love has one more name,
She calls it cocaine ...

If Only Both Heart Synchronize

All my promises were in red,
And so were the tears that were shed.
It felt much more than in between those two legs,
But it works if only both hearts synchronize…

Thy praises I sang night and day,
Life was blur but better this way,
Now you left and so did my smile,
Memories they ache and difficult to hide…

My eyes begged for nothing but you,
Now I just pretend they don't, but they still do,
And this madness that has come to stay,
Won't leave, though you have long walked away…

My youth is preserved in your apple smile,
And so often in your memory I write another line,
I can still feel you, but it doesn't feel the same,
Because it works if only both hearts synchronize…

Her Innocent Witchery

She is the room I lock myself in,
When I try to hide from my life.
It's her smile that I use,
To erase those unholy hours.
For she is the real gardener of my soul…

She gives me new pair of eyes,
To escape into another existence.
For she gives me surreal imagination,
To fill up my senses in vacant times…

It's her gift that I smile,
More often than I could.
It's her gift that I love,
More often than I would.
It's her gift that I believe in living,
More often than I should…

It's her innocent witchery that she practices on me,
And now I am drunk in the beauty of her ethereal existence.
Oh which street of madness have I been roaming?
And to wish away my youth in this way,
Dreaming about the promises of her smile,
And trying to read the meaning in between those lips.
But a single life spent, they say,
In her shadows is better,
Than a thousand lives of ignorance about her existence…

It's A Beautiful Day To Die

Everything will fall in place,
Everything that crawls in space.
There's nothing left but to replace,
All that changes has been blessed...

It's such a beautiful day to die today,
Nothing is coming my way,
No more pressure and nothing to say,
I think it's time for a summer spray...

The ray of sun on my bed naked and stray,
Everything has been said and done before,
And there is nothing much to live for,
It's a beautiful day to die today...

There is no measure to my pleasure,
Everything is perfect in my dreams,
And then when I wake up,
Everything goes back from where it springs,
Back in my head, where there is no fate,
Nothing to get up to and getting late,
And the future is you and everything's new,

It's a beautiful day to die today,
And go to a perfect world just made for me and you,
In my sleep, in my dreams…on my bed,
And my joy infectious in my head,
Cuts me open like a blade,
Smells like rose and your ribbon red,
And the pleasure is such a sudden rush of lust for more,
I pray I don't choke from an overdose,
It's a beautiful day to die today….

My Woman

These feelings that you leave unapologetically,
Are becoming difficult to hide.
Wish I could deny them but why should I?
Though it makes me feel restless but I feel alive…

I yield to every sensation that you give birth,
It lingers all day long and occupies my night.
I withdraw from my life as you fill up my senses,
What am I if not a puppet at your disposal?

I fear to lose you more than losing my life,
I wonder is there any difference between the two?
My fears may be unfound but still I fear,
And this fear is eating me to the point,
That I can't live without loving you even more…

I tried other ways to live and feel alive,
But nothing else tastes the same as you do.
So my woman so pretty come to me,
And share with me this space and time till eternity…

Zeynep

In between the words you say to me,
Those pauses of smile on your lips,
Don't do that so often,
Don't you know the way you look at me,
Controls my heartbeat...

I have been practicing your name hard,
So that I could say it to your face and talk,
But in those pretty pink ribbons,
And those tight little denims you wear,
When you walk up to me without any reason,
Don't you know, I just can't look you in those eyes and talk...

And when you talk to me,
Don't take my name so often,
Don't you know I keep a count of it,
And end up having sleepless nights over it...

And the memories of your childhood scar,
Photographs, dimples and glasses,
Recollection of the scent of your naked skin,
And after shower hair,
You should know and learn to forgive me,
For the innocent things I do to you inside my mind…

Sweet Acid Leaf

It might rain but I have some mushrooms,
A few drags more and I am mine,
Take my pipe to drain your pain,
I can fix you too with some glue,
If you come and share my leaf…

I got some Herbs, I need some bones,
From the graves of our past,
Let's burn some skeletons without soul,
Let's sniff some more gum and coal…

It might pain but here's some coke,
Got some needles in case you choke,
Some more pills to bring down the veil,
Why choose life when you can float…

I grew some grass, I got some seeds,
Got more blades to meet your needs,
Let's ride high on wax and some acid,
Hold my hand darling and we'll say a prayer,
Before we cut another layer…

For now I see the light through a leaf,
Through the smokes of relief,
See the clouds of my beliefs,
That's my life rolled up in a leaf…

Frau Gazeline

Her sleeping face,
The calmness of morning mist on a lake,
The mystic fog in the forest at dawn,
Waiting for its first kiss from sun,
And then the cloudless rain,
Falling from the stars at dawn,
Awakens her from her October slumber…

Oh her circle is pure,
Far beyond fear thinking,
Where my desires fear to tread,
But the silent call of her smile in spring,
Has invited me to surrender…

Her eyes are bottled wine,
The more you look into it,
The more you get drunk,
Some kind of witchcraft her beauty…

Please make me a part,
Of all your innocent rituals in red,
And then tie me up with your yellow knots,
Until I am sober in my head…

My Analogue Love

With your eyes blue,
Look into the blue,
As I look into you,
Don't break this silence,
This analogue,
This monologue of nothingness,
Let this silence play in loops,
Don't say a word,
What's in your heart,
Has already been heard.
Let's weave our self-tight,
In this ever growing silence
And as we pass into the night,
Lets watch the stars,
Hand in hand for hours,
And within this repetition of silence,
We quietly slip into sleep,
And wake up in our,
Darkest of desires,
Besides a fire,
In some forgotten shire.
Meet me eye to eye,

Let the feelings multiply,
No more fear, we are near,
Hand in hand,
Chained by love forever…

My Own Lover

I close my eyes and it opens within,
Let this enlightenment of senses prevail,
Of any friends I don't ask for,
Of a lover I don't beg.
I don't want the day to be perfect,
Nor the night to be merry.
I don't dream of a castle,
Or of a queen within.
I don't know of any habit that I have,
That can't be ended.
There are no bad memories that haunt me,
No good memories to hold on too.
Neither a giver of hope nor receiver of any.
Neither the seeker of the first dawn nor the last.
Neither the worshipper of number nor of any name.
All I want is to be my own lover,
Let me be my own first and the very last desire,
Make me so blind, like a moonless deep forest,
So that all I can do is look within,
Chain my hands and nail my legs,
So that the only place I can travel is deep within.
All I pray is to be my own liberator,

For no one shall enslave me but myself,
So I can find the me within me inside me.
All I pray is to be my own lover…

Petite Novelina

To each eyes that you comfort,
You mean something different.
As if a thousand lives that you have lived,
You could be anything to anyone.
I wonder how you would like to be remembered.
To me you are the sweet maiden,
Who is busy writing my life on paper.
Or are you a story I am living,
Through your dove like eyes…

You leave me craving for more every time,
I tip toe in the many worlds that you paint with words.
So write as much as you please,
For I shall read till it tires my soul,
And I will sleep on the lines of ink that you laid,
So I can wake up in your world where I long too…

Very contagious you are when you smile,
That sweetness dripping down your eyes,
Your butter coloured cheeks multiply your charm,
Have you been such a delight to watch all your life?

In fields of crops and green I see,
Your flowery figure dancing in the wind,
Your sun gilded hair in mild morning,
You mesmerize and then evaporate.
So often looking at you I feel,
Have I walked into a surreal dream?

Polygamous Monogamy

From one pain to another,
I walked down a path,
I thought I knew so well and how?
Another lover leaving without a goodbye…

The faces they keep changing,
But the pain remains the same,
And now years and years that follow,
They take shelter in my sorrow…

Oh another lover leaving without a goodbye,
Such a pain to see that my eyes bleed and cry,
But she looks so beautiful specially when I am in tears,
That I have long forgotten to smile over the years…

The taste of my love someday I know,
Would speak on her lips and turn them dry,
She would come calling,
Asking to love her more.
But if she ever calls me a bad lover,
I'll prove her wrong,
By loving, like a madman, someone another forever…

Condemned to Death By Life

So again we take this chance to blame,
This constant breathing has left us lame.
But suicide is a higher understanding of life,
And all that triumph is not life's defeat...

So we misuse again our right to hate,
The last judgment stares at our fate,
Preserver of revenge shall forfeit it again,
For we are condemned to death by life...

This lust is fresh right from our heart,
Every sin promises a brand new start,
To lie unpunished is not the nature's way,
To die without living is in vogue today...

Take farewell from all that is leaving now,
For survival is the essence of every lie,
And indifference shall possess the very living,
But some truth are only meant for royal taste,
And God for rabble and the waste...

Turkish Princess

The immortal stars make an intricate artwork,
Reminiscent of her eyes.
Carved with clockwork precision,
Her measures are so precise…

Like the wines in those cedar,
She never ages an inch,
For the time ages in place of her,
And so the musk ever present in the garden…

Those French poetries in air,
Are her whispers somewhere.
The silence she breaks with her smile,
And a thousand veils of sadness falls in my heart,
With just a glimpse of her…

I have died a million times,
Only to have taken birth again,
Just to solve the mystery that she is.
She is my secret,
That nobody will ever know or feel…

Roselyn

Roselyn come, let me walk you through,
The silent side of the moss hidden road,
That crawls lazily through the woods,
And disappears along with the lamppost in the fog ahead…

Roselyn come, let me show you the twilight star,
The moon without an inch of a scar,
At this time of year and hour,
November has never known to be this cold in rain,
But your scotch warm smile and memories old,
And the joy of nothing else to hold…

Roselyn it's the sweet scent,
Of the freshly brewed first rain soil,
Has it touched your soul sublime?
Open the umbrella that you hold,
I have reasons and some intention pure,
To feel the grace of thy skin porcelain,
Because what I feel now is beyond love, nameless…

Roselyn I want to do to you something dark,
That only our shadows will remember in silence,
Before we fade away along this,
Silent side of the moss hidden road,
That crawls lazily through the woods,
And disappears along with the lamppost in the fog
ahead…

My Shadow, My Widow

The pale shadows of my glorious past,
They search the silence seeking sonorous songs,
The serenade of the never born never died,
The laughter of the one's who never cried,
But now to the future my mind ever tied,
As I age half dead, without grace,
The triumph of the pills and the bills,
Shadow, my shadow, my widow,
Breathe in, breathe in and breathe out,
The signature of stigma as I vaporize in the sun,
Into the clouds, my grave, and then rebirth,
The rain brings me down again,
These rains, the tears of the many forgotten,
Gives way to a smile, a smile,
Growing from the bosom of earth,
Now I am feeding on this very rot,
And I recite by rote, I am the same old story,
Shadow, my shadow, my widow,
Where would you go when I am no more?

Princess Buttercup

A gentle reminder you are to my eyes,
Of the good luck charm that I need to survive,
And maybe I should collect all your memories,
For the times when the world treats me so cold…

It feels so warm inside when I look into your eyes,
There is no other place I would love to hide.
And if I could save these feelings for the years to follow,
Reality would be a bit easier to bear and swallow…

You are as elegant draped in silence and smile,
As you are when you choose words and voice,
And I walk besides you trying to capture your scent,
For my heart to battle the lonely hours…

I revisit my youth just to search for you,
How could I have missed knowing you for so long?
And now I surrender to your existence,
For I don't know what else to do with my life?

Her Meadows

Hearing her name for the first time,
I followed, not knowing where and why,
No matter how blind I was,
She led me through her heart,
Into a meadow,
Where her footfalls still echoes till today...

Hearing her voice for the first time,
I followed, with my innocence in dark,
No matter how blind I was,
She led me by the light of her eyes,
Into a meadow,
Where her smile made my heart pregnant with her love...

Hearing her whispers for the first time,
I followed, my first steps in love towards her,
She led me through the narrow red lanes of her lips,
Into a meadow,
Where my vacant eyes waited for her shadow...

There are a thousand ways to love that I know now,
And there are a thousand ways to kiss that I know now,
A thousand ways to kneel and hold hands in the dark,
But only one woman to feel all this for and that would be her…

Nirvajuana

So jealous of my loneliness,
Glad I feel the same again,
Naked in the crowd cold alone,
These clothes they hide no more,
How long am I going to carry this existence?
This living is an over hyped routine…

So I burnt some Apples for me again,
These medicines promise something new,
So I blew bubbles of green glue,
And all my dreams stuck to these bubbles and flew,
Never been so fun drowning in the blue…

So I blew more bubbles of green glue,
And now the grass is green on my side,
There is a silence that uses words I hear,
And I see laughter in every tear,
Look at those Jelly fishes raining from the clouds,
Look at those blank walls talking so loud,
These feelings are more than sexual,
It's pure intellectual technicolor orgasm…

Now the grass is green on my side,
I waited but you never came,
I fear I might not need you anymore,
I'll grow more company in my backyard,
I'll breed more friends inside my head,
I'll take them to bed without begging,
I fear I might not fear life anymore…

I'm so jealous of my loneliness,
I'm glad I feel the same again,
Naked in the crowd cold alone,
These clothes they hide no more,
How long am I going to carry this existence?
This living is an over hyped routine…

Rubina Yousufsai

My fair maiden don't ask,
Don't ask me about my art.
You know better what I suffer from,
It's your gift, your grace,
Take it away anytime you want,
The words flow when you dance inside my heart.
Just like the ink and paper,
I am just a medium of expression of your beauty...

My fair maiden don't ask,
Don't ask me if I am a mad man.
In the light of your beauty,
I see things unseen before.
I hear voices from the world that you belong.
Don't ask me my maiden if I am a mad man,
You know better what I suffer from...

Oh fair maiden don't ask,
Don't ask me what time is it,
I am in a daze,
Ever since I got drunk by your gaze,
I stopped keeping time ever since our eyes met,
This stupor was the bliss I was searching for.
My consciousness now just clings to your existence of the purest form…

Ramona Osbourne

She walks into the best of my dreams,
And makes me pregnant with life,
With all those alibis in her eyes,
And those nonchalant harmless humour,
That she unleashes to kill her time,
Oh I just get drawn into her circle…

She colonizes me with her eyes and breath,
And everything that comes out of her head,
I just love to watch her innocence play,
And given half a chance I would sell all my dreams,
To be a passing reference in her pages…

She hardly cares about her,
Just out of the bed school girl innocence,
And those braided blonde musk double ponytails,
Begging to be smelled over and over again,
I wonder do those lips ever go dry, the cups of nectar…

Lady I know for sure you practice extra hard,
To be that humble and naive,
For if I was even half as beautiful as you,
I'd count the stars as my admirers too,
For your pure bloodline belongs to heaven…

Inside Your Head

Open your arms grandiose,
Embrace this fall from grace,
Its just your eternal pain,
And the triumph of solitude again…

A pledge of hope, a pledge of patience,
We are victims of our own contradiction,
Renew the orgasm of ignorance,
And follow the promise of peace…

It's just the rule of living,
Another reign shall end soon,
And forgotten before next begins.
Illusion of purpose has served us well,
Unbroken in this life and the next…

Questions to Yulia

Do those tattoos keep you safe?
Or the photographs of your mother you carry?
Do you still love being called by the name your father gave?
Have those early morning prayers brought you peace?

Do you still prefer those baby blue sweaters,
Red umbrellas and yellow hair?
Do you still wear the same old summer fragrance that haunts me?
Or have you changed it for the man you have coffee with?

Do you still prefer those fairytales over sacred verses?
Does God still forgive you in return for your innocent smile?
Do you still fight those tears with sun glasses on?
Are dark chocolates and flowers still a cure for your mood swings?

Do you still hug those pillows tight on rainy nights?
Have those winter experiments with Vodka and Wine kept you warm?
Have you started getting Beethoven right on sunday mornings?
Or do you still miss those black keys on G minor?

All that remains of you is just a voice now,
Running in loops inside my head,
Lingers like a shadow and then fades,
By which name should I love you now?
In which face should I find you now?

Monarchy of the Fallen

Constant prayers for desires undying,
Awakens the long melancholy from sleep,
And the forgotten monarchy of the fallen,
Shall see the last supper of mirth…

Worship the withered, Leave alone the grief,
There is wisdom in nature's prudence.
These emotions are our own conclusion…

So betray the tyranny of reason,
Uphold the anarchy of heart,
And axe the frozen lake within.
Kiss this feeling fading slowly,
Before you lay forgotten…

Morning Innocence

She wears a mask of morning innocence,
Which brightens up with the first drop from sun,
Her face the very essence of rose,
Her life an eternal immortal prose.
She is a holy sign from God,
Love her if you want to be in heaven…

Life is an art,
She practices very hard,
Ever absence of any blunder,
And even in winter I wonder,
How she manages to blossom,
When the whole world sleeps,
Under earth's bosom…

She is the translation of silence,
A symphony of the sea,
She is best understood without words,
Like the prefigure of spring,
She is a meaning never heard…

She robs me of my imagination,
The symptoms are clear when she is near,
My eyes won't allow me to speak,
Its even hard to describe her sins,
Oh the August child and her innocence…

Reticent Patchwork

Of all that rotten has plagued my mind,
But still smiling amongst the ruins,
Of the rust of past that settles around,
My optimism multiplying now and sadness dying…

Silence that sleeps in the heart of the dead,
Was once bled to death in the chains of hope,
In the utopian fields of loneliness.
And now I am victim of my own conscience,
Insulate me from my flaws and my kind…

Beneath the veneer of happiness,
A common ugliness lay dormant,
The constant future's shadow looms,
On the minds of the living…

See the patchwork of reticent autumn,
And this interplay of springtime light,
But when the spell of what's real is broken,
It's just your illusion surreal…

And when all that fades,
Shall bless your existence,
The repetition of guilt will stop,
By revealing everything you hide again,
In the open arms of eternal innocence...

Grow On Me

You know I am so used to you,
I can't grow on anyone else.
My roots are deep inside your heart,
And I blossom with your every touch,
Sweetest flower, I am your Bee,
I pollinate you with love,
And drink all your nectar.
Grow on me as I grow on you…

And you do know,
All the efforts I take to please you,
It has all become a habit now.
Days feel empty and nights vacant,
If I don't serve you right,
For I am slave to all your desires.
There are infinite ways to love you,
And to love you in every possible way,
I need to hurry for I fear to run out of life.
For I know I am dealing with a princess here,
So teach me how to love you best,
Grow on me as I grow on you…

To think of me only in terms of you,
And to love you in ways obscure,
Keeper of all your words I am,
That are born from your beautiful mouth.
Paint me with all your emotions,
Vomit in me as much as you please,
I am your dustbin my lady,
Use me at your ease.
And as I read to you from stars in bed,
I beg to you all over again, please!
Grow on me as I grow on you…

Petite Neslihan

And petite Neslihan,
She must have won all the battles of her life,
For she can be anything she wants,
She must have won all the battles of love too,
For she is so strong…

And petite Neslihan,
She is the confession of God that love still exists,
She is the prophecy of wandering Dervishes,
A promise of spring to return back in time,
She is the scent that Mother Earth loves to wear in rain,
Everything about her is like the sweetness of Urdu and
bewitching Ittar,
She can be anything to my dreaming mind,
She is the world when I close my eyes.
Oh she is love…

And petite Neslihan,
She is the smile on the face of Earth,
A child of Renaissance,
God took more time to carve her than you and me,
She can be anything to anyone,
She is the Eden in blossom,

The pleasure is to watch her, Not to touch,
For I fear to pollute the divine,
Oh she is an art unfolding…

Morning Gospel

The dawn's darling light has come to call,
We wake up to the faded fallen stars,
But in victor's coffin our ego sleep,
One day the life will break this myth…

Every memory either good or bad,
Makes us a slave of an ever increasing past,
But bondage is life's eternal message,
The real freedom is in her chains…

Hope is the poison we drink to live,
As we breathe and gift ourselves another day,
Through clock watch it fade away,
And what difference did it ever make?
Today is tomorrow and yesterday is yesterday…